5/11

°/11 ox

CR

COLONIAL PEOPLE

The Silversmith

WIL MARA

 **Marshall Cavendish**
Benchmark
New York

Library of Congress Cataloging-in-Publication Data

Mara, Wil.
The silversmith / by Wil Mara.
p. cm. — (Colonial people)
Includes bibliographical references and index.
Summary: "Explore the life of a colonial silversmith and his importance to the community, as well as everyday life,
responsibilities, and social practices during that time"—Provided by publisher.
ISBN 978-0-7614-4804-4
1. Silversmiths—United States—History—18th century—Juvenile literature. 2. Silverwork, Colonial—United States—History—
18th century—Juvenile literature. 3. United States—History—Colonial period, ca. 1600–1775—Juvenile literature. I. Title.
HD8039.S5262U663 2011
739.2'3097309033—dc22
2009035563

Editor: Christine Florie
Publisher: Michelle Bisson
Art Director: Anahid Hamparian
Series Designer: Kay Petronio

Expert Reader: James H. Williams, Professor of History and Director of the
Albert Gore Research Center, Middle Tennessee State University, Murfreesboro

Photo research by Marybeth Kavanagh
Cover photo by The Granger Collection, NY
The photographs in this book are used by permission and through the courtesy of: *North Wind Picture Archives*: 4, 7;
The Bridgeman Art Library: Private Collection, 9; Historic New England, Boston, Massachusetts, USA, 14;
Virginia Historical Society, Richmond, Virginia, USA, 22; *Corbis*: Freelance Photography Guild, 10; Ted Spiegel,
13; Bettmann, 32; *Chris Graham*: 16; *Alamy*: Irene Abdou, 20; *The Colonial Williamsburg Foundation*: 24, 31;
The Image Works: Irene Abdou, 27; *The Granger Collection, NY*: 38

Printed in Malaysia (T)
1 3 5 6 4 2

CONTENTS

ONE

Colonial Times in America

In the early to mid–1600s, Europeans began taking ships to North America by the thousands. Some had hopes of making a better life for themselves. Others were in search of religious freedom. Their plan was to set up new communities in the New World, called colonies. Thus, they became known as colonists.

These brave and courageous people traveled across the open seas on wooden ships that were often old and leaky. Many vessels sank before ever reaching American shores. Illness was common on board. One sick person on a ship sometimes meant many others got sick, too. This was a time when illness could not be cured easily. Smallpox, influenza, and many other diseases that are treatable today swept through colonial communities, killing many.

In 1607 Englishmen arrived on the shores of what is now the State of Virginia and established the settlement of Jamestown.

The hardship did not end when these travelers reached America. They had to get to work clearing land and building homes to protect themselves from harsh weather. Also, a colony could be attacked at any time by American Indians in areas where colonists had turned the native peoples into enemies. The American Indians had been living in North America when the colonists first arrived. After an early period of peaceful relations, the American Indians became unhappy about having to share their land.

Still, the colonists kept on, and soon their hard work paid off. Small villages grew into towns, and some towns grew into cities. As the colonists built homes and farms, they also put up schools, churches, and places of business. Many of the early colonists were farmers; but soon there were teachers, innkeepers, bakers, blacksmiths, carpenters, masons, and others.

American Silversmithing Begins

One of America's first big cities was Boston. It grew on the shores of a northern colony called Massachusetts. This was where silversmithing began in colonial times. Most of the best silversmiths who came from Europe lived there. Silversmithing was a good business in Boston. Many of the wealthiest colonists lived in and around the Boston area—and they bought plenty of silver.

Silversmithing began in the colonial city of Boston, Massachusetts.

Also, a lot of business—including the sale of silver items—was done with European customers by way of ships that arrived in Boston Harbor. In time Boston silversmiths became known for the high quality of their work.

Silver, like gold, became valuable because it was considered a treasure among American colonists. Silver coins, for example, had much greater worth than paper money. Paper money was often regarded as nothing more than what it was made of: paper. Silver, however, could be used to make other things besides coins, including jewelry, household ornaments, and eating utensils (such as forks, knives, and spoons).

Silver was rare in colonial days. It was **mined** by slaves in Mexico and South America and then sent back to Europe, where it was used to pay for wars and to set up new colonies around the world. The European governments that ruled these colonies did not want the colonists to have too much silver, though. It gave them power and wealth, which made them harder to govern. When colonists asked for more silver coins to be sent over, they were ignored. There was also a law that said the colonists were not allowed to make their own silver coins. This law was broken in 1652 when the first American mint was built in Boston.

Silver was also a smart way for colonists to protect their wealth. There were no savings banks in the early colonial days, and paper money, as well as coins, was stolen all the time. Many silver items, however, were large and heavy, and therefore difficult to steal. Also, they usually had the initials of someone's name imprinted on them: either that of the owner or of the silversmith who made them.

A Growing Trade

Due to silver's increasing popularity, silversmiths began opening shops in parts of America beyond Boston. They also began to advertise their talents in order to get customers. One silversmith from South Carolina put the following ad in his local newspaper—

*James Rutherford, a regular bred gold and silversmith, just arrived from Edinburg, makes and mends all kinds of **plate**, and other work in his business, after the best and newest fashions, on reasonable terms.*

America's colonial era ended in July 1776 with the adoption of

Silver was a popular metal in colonial America. As the demand for silver items grew, so did the need for silversmiths.

A Silversmith
Who Made History

Paul Revere is one of the most famous people in American history. He is best known for his midnight ride from Boston to Lexington, Massachusetts, in April 1775. His job was to warn John Hancock and Samuel Adams—two of the men leading the fight for America's independence during the Revolutionary War—that British soldiers were coming to capture them.

What many people do not know is that Revere made his living as a silversmith. Paul Revere's silver business was started by Paul's father, who taught his son the secrets of silversmithing. When his father died in 1754, Paul was still too young to take over the business. Instead, he became a lieutenant in the army and fought in the **French and Indian War**. After the war he came back to the shop and, now old enough, began his silversmithing career. He became one of the finest smiths of his time, and today his pieces are considered great treasures.

the famous Declaration of Independence. That was when the colonies declared that they were no longer under the control of the British government. The art of American silversmithing was well under way at this point and would continue to develop far into the future.

TWO

The Silversmith

Not everyone could become a silversmith. Although a silversmith had to have skilled hands, he also needed a combination of patience, experience, discipline, and focus. A blacksmith could make a hammer or fix an ax without too much concern for detail. A silversmith, however, might spend hours simply **engraving** a spoon or shaping a mug handle. He knew his customers would inspect every inch of his creations.

What It Took to Be a Silversmith

A silversmith had to have the ability to work with silver (and sometimes other precious metals, as well). He had to know how to melt it, how to form it into different shapes, how to create different designs with it, how to cut engravings into it, and so on. This knowledge came about only after years of learning and practice.

The colonial silversmith took much pride in his work as he created quality items for his customers.

Since silver was expensive, the silversmith had very little room to make mistakes. The best silversmiths were those who took their time and fully focused their attention on each piece. They understood that the creation of beautiful things could not be rushed, because rushing led to sloppy work.

The style of silver items changed from year to year. A good silversmith kept up with the trends, creating pieces popular for the day. This mug (left), minature tankard (center), and cann (right) were created by a colonial Boston silversmith.

A silversmith also had to understand the importance of **reputation**. Since silver was so valuable and beloved, a silversmith's customers had to believe they would always get an honest deal. If, for example, a silversmith said a bowl was made from 10 ounces of silver, then it had to be exactly 10 ounces. Also, a silversmith would be judged on the quality of his work, because no one wanted to pay for something ugly or poorly made.

A silversmith also had to know what styles were popular. In England, for example, perhaps salt and pepper shakers had floral designs on the sides. Or maybe candlesticks went from being very fancy one year to being very simple the next. A silversmith had to know what his customers would be looking for and then adjust his designs to suit the tastes of the day.

Churches—Another Big Customer

While wealthy people were perhaps a silversmith's most common customer, church leaders were probably a close second. People who went to church were asked to give a small amount of their money as a means of supporting the church. These donations allowed churches to buy fine silver items such as candlesticks, plates, and cups to use during worship services. Church leaders did not care as much about fashion or style as a silversmith's other customers. Some of the colonial silver pieces found in churches today are among the oldest in America.

Most silversmiths worked long, hard days. Silver items were time-consuming to make. It was not unusual for a silversmith to work twelve hours in a single day. Many smiths also worked six days a week instead of five. If a silversmith fell behind with his orders, he might have to work well into the night.

Acquiring Raw Silver

Since it was nearly impossible to import bars of silver from Europe, most of the silver used by colonial silversmiths came either from coins or, oddly enough, silver items that had already been made. A silversmith's shop might have piles of cups, pots, bowls, forks, knives, hairbrushes, mirrors, and dozens of other items sitting in a wooden crate, waiting to be melted down. In his book *The Colonial Silversmith: His Techniques and His Products*, author Henry J. Kauffman says that "the metal of the silversmith was obtained by melting down coins or

Silver was sometimes hard to get, so colonial silversmiths would melt old silver items to create new ones.

re-melting earlier objects which were outdated in style." The author comments, "The ruthless destruction of early masterpieces by American silversmiths is . . . unfortunate." Apparently, however, the silversmiths who made these "earlier objects" did not mind them being destroyed, for the author then says that "the craftsmen were willing partners in this catastrophe."

Colonial silversmiths always mixed copper with their silver. This was not dishonest as long as the amount of copper was kept low. Silversmith **guilds** did not allow any silver item to have more than 7.5 percent copper (which meant the remaining 92.5 percent had to be pure silver). Silver of this type is called sterling. There are almost no known silver items from colonial times that broke this rule.

Learning the Trade

A silversmith was not, of course, born with the knowledge he needed for his craft—he had to learn it. And the most common way to do this was to become an apprentice. An apprentice was a teenager or young man who spent a number of years working with an experienced silversmith—called a master—in order to learn the trade. The hope was that the apprentice would eventually become a master as well. Since most children in colonial America had little schooling, apprenticeship was the main way young people learned a skill or trade that could become a job when they were adults. Because of beliefs at the time, girls could not apprentice to become silversmiths. Instead, their apprenticeship took place in households, where they were taught to be good wives and mothers when they were old enough to marry and start families.

In Europe an apprentice often paid a silversmith for the right to learn silversmithing. In colonial America, however, a silversmith often allowed a young man to be his apprentice for free. This was because there simply were not as many people living in America as in Europe, and the silversmith was happy to have someone helping him in his shop each day.

An apprentice would sometimes have to sign a contract. The apprentice agreed to behave himself and do as he was told. One silversmith contract that was written in July 1719 said that the apprentice "faithfully shall serve his Secretts keep his lawfull Commands gladly, Every where obey." An apprentice was expected to be honest, too, since he would be working with a very valuable metal as well as valuable tools. The same contract said that the apprentice "shall not waste his Masters Goods nor lend them unlawfully to any." As part of the contract, he was often given food, clothing, and even a place to live. An apprenticeship was supposed to last seven years on average, but most lasted about four or five.

Most apprentices were young boys. As such, they sometimes got into trouble. For example, some lost interest in silversmithing and made their masters angry by not paying attention. Others might frequently be late for work or not show up at all. A master might even arrive at his shop to discover some of his silver gone—and never see his apprentice again. Ads often appeared in colonial newspapers telling local people to be on the lookout for such thieves. If caught, dishonest apprentices would be severely punished.

An apprentice rarely had his own set of tools. Instead, he had to use his master's. As the years passed, however, a master might buy (or make) new tools for himself and give his old ones to his apprentice. Or he might teach the apprentice how to make his own. Making tools from scratch was common in colonial times. Many silversmiths preferred to make their own, as they wanted their tools to be exactly to their liking.

The master decided when an apprenticeship was finished. He might sign a note or letter saying that the young man was now a master, too. Sometimes the master would first ask his apprentice to make one last silver item to prove his skill. This piece, usually

An apprentice would use his master's tools as he learned the trade.

called an apprentice piece, had to be of the same high quality as any of the master's pieces.

At the end of an apprenticeship, the new master had two choices. The first was to stay with his former master and work in his shop. The second was to move away in search of a new town— one that did not already have a silversmith. Then he would set up a shop of his own. A person who made this choice was called a **journeyman**. Before the journeyman went on his way, his former master might give him a new set of clothes and some money.

Other Talents of a Silversmith

Many silversmiths did more than just hammer out silver bowls and spoons all day. Some also did repair work. In colonial times metal of all kinds could be very expensive. The same held true for any precious items made from silver; if the handle on a bowl or the tine of a fork broke off, for example, the owner did not even think about throwing away the item. The person would simply bring it back to the silversmith to have it repaired.

Most silversmiths were also skilled engravers. *Engraving* means cutting intricate designs or handsome lettering into metal. It was difficult work. The best engravers had to have a steady

A skilled colonial silversmith engraved this silver badge in the mid–1600s in Virginia.

hand and a keen eye—and plenty of patience. It was slow, delicate work. But it also paid off: a silversmith who engraved well would always have plenty of customers.

THREE

Inside a Silversmith's Shop

The shop of a silversmith was designed for working rather than selling. It was a place where beautiful things were created—but where the process of creating those things was often messy and exhausting.

On the Outside

The earliest American silversmiths did not have their own shops. Instead, they worked from a room in their home. Since they needed very hot fire to melt silver, the workroom would have a small stone **furnace**. Sometimes the furnace was built outside for safety.

Eventually a silversmith might build a separate place on his property, such as a small shed. As larger towns and cities eventually developed in colonial America, many silversmiths

A silversmith tends the furnace in this re-created shop in Williamsburg, Virginia.

realized it would be a good idea to open shops there. In the most prosperous years for the colonies, just before the American Revolution began, people came to the cities by the thousands—all ready to spend their money.

A smart silversmith would hang a sign in front of his shop. Usually the sign would say something simple, such as JEREMIAH JONES, SILVERSMITH. The sign was cut in the shape of a common silver item, such as a bowl or a teapot. The shape of the sign was not just for decoration; it meant that the shop belonged to a silversmith.

A clever silversmith would also put his most beautiful items in the front window, where people walking by would notice them. When they stepped inside, there would be even more beautiful items to see. Many silversmiths had to build a wall between the display area and the place where they worked. A silversmith's workshop could be very hot, dirty, and smoky.

The Tools of a Silversmith

A silversmith had dozens of different tools. Each one did something the others did not, so they were all important. As noted in the book *The Colonial Silversmith: His Techniques and His Products*, "Each silversmith had his favorite tools for doing specific jobs and the loss of one was regarded as a catastrophe."

Perhaps the most common tool was the hammer. A silversmith used different hammers to beat silver into various shapes. The difference between hammers was the size and shape of their heads: one might be large and flat, whereas another would be small and rounded. Some had a circular shape; others were square. When creating a silver bowl, a silversmith might use a large hammer to whack the silver into its rough bowl shape. He would use a smaller hammer to gently tap out the fine details of the bowl's rim.

Shears were a silversmith's scissors. They were used to cut sheets of plain silver into various shapes. They were made of tough iron, and their blades had to be kept very sharp to cut the silver smoothly and easily. Smaller shears, often called snips, were used to make very tiny cuts, sometimes as part of finely detailed work.

An anvil is a large block of iron with a long point sticking out of one side (sometimes two). The silversmith would set the silver on the anvil, shaping the metal while at the same time striking it with his hammers.

Tongs are similar to scissors in design, but they are used to pick up things rather than to cut them. They also act like metal fingers when picking up items that are very hot. For example, if a silver bar had to be heated before hammering could begin, the silversmith

The silversmith used different kinds of hammers to create a variety of shapes.

Tool Care

A silversmith could not do anything without his tools, so the tools always had to be kept in good condition. A hammer that had a chip or a scratch in its head, for example, would leave marks on the silver. Also, many of a silversmith's tools were made of iron, which meant that they would rust if left in a damp place.

Tools were expensive in colonial times. If a tool became broken or rusty, a silversmith probably would not throw it out and buy a new one. Broken tools could always be fixed, but that took time and cost money. Better was the idea of taking great care of them in the first place. Some tools were wrapped in soft cloth when they were not being used. They might be kept on a high shelf where no one could get to them. Some might even be kept in containers of oil or animal fat. Doing this made it impossible for the tools to develop rust.

would set the bar in his furnace with a pair of tongs. Later he would use the tongs again to remove the hot bar.

A silversmith could not have done much without a furnace. A furnace is similar to an ordinary fireplace except that it gets much hotter. Extreme heat was created with the help of a bellows. When the handles of the bellows were pushed together, air was forced through a pointed tube at the other end. When a smith blew hard on a fire with bellows, the heat in the furnace rose to very high levels, and the silver could be melted.

FOUR

The Life of a Silversmith

A silversmith's day usually started early and ended late. The hours were long, and the work could be very hard. A silversmith might also have to deal with problems that made the work more difficult. Sometimes there was not enough silver to make all the items that he wanted. Or maybe he did not have enough people helping him in the shop. Every now and then an important tool would break and need to be fixed or melted down and made again. A silversmith had to find ways to work around these problems in order to keep his business going.

Creating Something from Silver

The first step for a silversmith was to melt the silver he needed. He would use either silver items that he had bought from people who did not want them anymore or coins that were common in colonial times. Most of these coins were from European countries and included Spanish dollars and pesos, Portuguese crusadoes, and English crowns and shillings.

All silver would be placed into the furnace—along with a small and carefully measured amount of copper—in a container called a **crucible**. A crucible was usually made of graphite. Graphite is tougher than silver and will not melt at the same high temperature.

After the silver was melted, the silversmith poured the molten metal into a mold.

A flat disk of silver is hammered into a bowl.

A crucible was often long and rectangular. That was so the silver, after it cooled, would be in the shape of a bar. This bar is called an ingot.

A silversmith would set an ingot aside until he needed it. When it came time to use the ingot, a piece of it might be cut off and put back into the furnace to be turned into liquid again. Then the silver was poured into a pan. If the pan was round, the silver would cool into the shape of a large disk. The silversmith could easily hammer the disk into the shape of a bowl or a teapot. If he was making a mug, he might instead pour the silver into a square or rectangular pan. When the silver cooled, he could bend the sheet into the shape of a tube. This became the body of the mug.

Shaping a piece of silver into a beautiful design, with every little detail, took many hours. The silversmith often had to put the silver back into the furnace for a short time to keep it soft. It was then

Making His Mark

Once an item was properly shaped and put together, the silversmith would stamp his initials into it. Just about every colonial silversmith had a special design for his initials. Some put letters inside a circle or a heart. Others included tiny pictures of animals or trees. Aside from making a piece with his initials, a silversmith might also engrave the name of the person for whom he made the item.

easier to tap and knock it into just the right shape. It was also good for a smith to have a model from which to work: a piece that was already finished and could be copied.

Sometimes the different parts of a silver item had to be put together like a puzzle. For example, a silversmith might make a teapot in four separate pieces: handle, spout, lid, and body. The spout and the handle would be attached to the body by a process called soldering. Brass was added to make the **solder** stronger. When the solder cooled down and became hard, it acted as a kind of superglue. Sometimes, instead, two pieces were connected with rivets: small pins that could be used like nails to hold one piece on to another.

The last step in making a silver item was to polish it until it had a perfect shine.

Cleaning Silver Made Easy, and Fun

Silver sometimes becomes tarnished—it loses its shine and becomes quite dull. If you have any silver items in your house that could use a cleaning, here is a fun and easy way to do it. However, please note that you *must* have an adult help you with this activity.

Things You Will Need

- Boiling water
- A pan or bowl large enough to hold the silver completely underwater
- A sheet of aluminum foil
- The tarnished silver item
- Baking soda
- A soft towel or cloth

Instructions

1. Have an adult begin boiling the water—you will need enough to fully cover the silver item once it has been placed in the pan or bowl.

2. Line the bottom of the pan or bowl with the sheet of aluminum foil.

3. Set the silver item on the aluminum foil (make sure it is touching the foil).

4. Once the water is boiling, have the adult pour it into the pan or bowl until the silver item is completely immersed.

5. Add the baking soda. The correct amount is about 1 cup of baking soda per gallon of water. The baking soda may begin to fizz as soon as it's added. This is normal. After a few moments, watch as the tarnish on the silver gradually begins to disappear.

6. Once all the tarnish is gone, have the adult pour out the water/baking soda mixture, then cool down the silver item by running some cold water on it.

7. Dry off the silver item with a soft towel or cloth. If the item is not nice and shiny after one treatment, do one more. Two is enough to clean off most tarnish.

Getting Paid

Every now and then a customer might try to talk a silversmith into lowering his prices. A man who had been silversmithing for a long time would expect this and know how to deal with it. While the customer would give reasons for a lower price, the silversmith would give reasons why the price should *not* be lowered. This practice of back-and-forth arguing over money is called **haggling**, and it was fairly common in colonial days.

In poorer areas where coins were scarce, a silversmith might not get any money at all. Instead, he might get **farm pay** for his work. For example, if a smith made a set of wedding bands or other jewelry for a farm family, he might receive a pig, a barrel of cider, or a few bags of apples in return.

FIVE

A Smith and His Community

Many of the people who bought items from a colonial silversmith were wealthy. Having silver in their homes was a way of showing off their high place in the community. This meant the silversmith knew the wealthy people in his town fairly well. He had to be trusted by them, and he had to be known as someone who did excellent work. For colonists in the middle and lower classes, a silversmith might produce plates, tankards, or other sturdy household items, often making them out of pewter instead of silver, as pewter was more common and less expensive.

One of the Better "Mechanicks"

In colonial times most people were farmers. This was largely because growing food was so important in early America: if people did not have food, they could not eat. The second most common type of workers were craftsmen and artisans: people who worked with their hands but were not farmers. These included carpenters, coopers, blacksmiths, and, of course, silversmiths. As one large group, they were often called **mechanicks**. Mechanicks were, for the most part, lower to middle class. They rarely rose above the middle class into the wealthy, upper class. They could make a good living if they worked hard, but it was unusual for them to become truly rich.

Owning silver was a sign of wealth. Paul Revere created this silver tea set for one of his well-to-do customers in Boston.

Silversmiths were thought of as the better part of the mechanicks group. They were usually very intelligent and very patient. Sometimes they were educated, too. If they had a good reputation, they could indeed earn a nice living. Perhaps most importantly, they produced items of great beauty. A blacksmith might have the ability to make an ax or a door hinge, but these were everyday items. They did not show off a person's wealth (or the creative talents that many blacksmiths possessed). A silversmith, however, created objects that could be admired and appreciated. Also, a blacksmith worked mostly with iron, which was not considered a precious metal.

High Respect and Regard

In colonial times being honest and trustworthy was very important. Individuals who could not be trusted did not get very far in their communities. They were considered low people to be avoided. Most silversmiths were thought of in just the opposite way: they were given the greatest regard. They worked with silver, after all, which was considered the same as money. In this sense, they were among America's first bankers. To give a silversmith your silver was to trust him fully. Silver was of great worth both in monetary terms and in social status. It was not hastily handed over to someone else.

And because silversmiths did such difficult and finely detailed work, they were highly respected.

When Jeremiah Dummer, one of Boston's greatest silversmiths, died in May 1718, the newspapers remembered him as "having served his country faithfully, in several Publick Stations, and obtained of all that knew him the Character of a Just, Virtuous, and Pious-Man." Another was Joseph Richardson, who died in November 1770. The local newspaper called him "a Gentleman whose private virtues, and public spirit justly claimed the friendship, esteem, and confidence of his fellow citizens and others."

Many silversmiths were able to hold important positions in their communities. They were invited to join councils that made decisions regarding the town's growth and development. They became members of clubs that were not open to just anybody. Sometimes they married women from wealthy and powerful families. If a man got to know the right kind of people, he could move up in his community fairly quickly as a silversmith.

The Silversmith's Legacy

Silversmiths were among colonial America's first truly great craftsmen. From the earliest days in Boston until the signing of the

The Case of Samuel Casey

Not *all* silversmiths were known for their honesty and virtue. Consider the sad case of Samuel Casey. Born in Newport, Connecticut, in the late 1600s, he grew to become one of the colonies' most honored silversmiths. His work was always interesting because he would try out new styles and designs that other silversmiths would not. His home caught fire one night, causing Casey to lose just about everything he owned.

He moved to the nearby town of Little Rest and began using his smithing skills again. This time, however, it was for something terrible: making counterfeit money. Casey was soon caught and confessed to the crime. Then he was brought into a courtroom, where he was judged guilty and sentenced to be hung. However, the night before his hanging, a crowd of his friends came to the jail and set him free. He was never heard from again—but he still holds a place in American history as one of the few known dishonest silversmiths.

Declaration of Independence in July 1776, American silversmiths had a reputation for making products of outstanding quality. Few people knew how much time and hard work went into the creation of a silver plate or creamer. The smith trained and practiced for years before he mastered his trade. Many young men tried to become silversmiths and failed—which meant only the best succeeded. Today, the many pieces of American silver that survive from the colonial era are considered works of art. They are also reminders of people who were talented, hardworking, and trustworthy: all the qualities that carried America through its difficult colonial period and would serve it well in the years ahead.

Glossary

crucible	a container for holding molten (liquid) metal
engrave	to cut a design or character (a letter or number) into metal
farm pay	something that is given in trade instead of money
French and Indian War	the war fought in North America in the mid–1700s between the British and the combined forces of France and various American-Indian tribes
furnace	a place where extreme heat is made for the purpose of melting or softening metal
guild	an association of merchants or artisans organized to maintain standards and protect its members
haggle	to argue over the price of something
journeyman	a former apprentice who has left his master to seek work elsewhere
mechanick	a colonial-era term used to describe anyone who, by trade, works with their hands
mine	a hole in the earth from which silver and other metals and minerals can be taken
plate	a colonial-era term used to describe any item made by a silversmith
reputation	the way a person is thought of by others
solder	liquefied metal used to connect two metal parts

Find Out More

BOOKS

Hazen, Walter. *Colonial Times*. Tucson, AZ: Good Year Books, 2008.

Johnson, Terri (compiler). *What Really Happened in Colonial Times*. Mississauga, ON, Canada: Knowledge Quest Books, 2007.

Kalman, Bobby. *A Visual Dictionary of a Colonial Community*. New York: Crabtree Publishing, 2008.

Petersen, Christine. *The Blacksmith*. New York: Marshall Cavendish Benchmark, 2010.

Roberts, Russell. *Life in Colonial America*. Hockessin, DE: Mitchell Lane Publishers, 2007.

WEBSITES

Social Studies for Kids

www.socialstudiesforkids.com/subjects/colonialtimes.htm

This site offers many excellent links to information on the life and times of the colonists in early America.

Kid Info

www.kidinfo.com/American_History/Colonization_Colonial_Life.html

This website features many helpful links to useful information on colonial life.

Colonial Williamsburg

www.history.org/kids/games/

The games and activities page on the Colonial Williamsburg site has many fun and interesting things to do, all of educational value.

Index

About the Author

Wil Mara has written more than a hundred books, many of which are educational titles for young readers. A full bibliography of his work can be found at www.wilmara.com.